'INVITE THE DIVINE'

POEMS

SHAKIL A I DAWOOD

KINDLE DIRECT PUBLISHING

'INVITE THE DIVINE'

THE POEMS

Of Difficulty then the Joy, are part of the Aspects of the Heart Series Volume 24.

Cover: Science and Medicine:
Dental and Vision: The Eye
Courtesy and thanks to
Kindle Direct Publishing, RF Image.

This volume of verse is dedicated to my friend Ron Berisha, for his tremendous kindness, understanding and support for me.

FIRST EDITION

LONDON JANUARY 2022

KINDLE DIRECT PUBLISHING

Shakil Ahmed Ismail Dawood has had London made his home for nearly five decades now, hailing originally from Nairobi, Kenya. He schooled and then went to university in London, graduating in Environmental Studies and Geography in 1986.

Literature had always been a life-long interest and he began actively writing poetry at the age of thirty-three. Shakil has published many volumes of general verse as well as writing poetry on schizophrenia and psychosis. He has also written a self-help book on the subject of depression.

Shakil sees Art as a primal expression and experience of human beings, and vital and critical to their rejuvenation and resurrection from the current impasse humanity finds itself in today. An expanded inner dimension will be absolutely necessary if we are to do this and Art offers a true and authentic possibility of this inward movement and development.

Introduction

Writing this volume of verse came out of a habitual occupation of my own – the need and necessity of emerging from a constantly present trough like existence of difficulties.

These poems show some of these experiences and a constant battle waged against adversity. In each instance, I did not give up the quest for catharsis and solace: and in each instance, I emerged head high, for in speaking ultimately, I was utilizing the greatest human qualities to tackle my issues: patience, love, goodness and kindness.

I have written this book to portray the fact that any battle conducted with sincerity and a longing for good character will not fail. Goodwill and goodness are uppermost qualities: this perhaps is my ultimate message, more particularly to a troubled world which is seeking answers to imperative dilemmas.

Shakil Ahmed Ismail Dawood,
April 2021.

'INVITE THE DIVINE'

THE POEMS

INVITE THE DIVINE INTO YOUR LIFE…

Invite the Divine
Into your life
If disabled:

I had bestowed
Upon me
Unparalleled hardship
The adversity
Of disability

However,
Disability,
Taken well,
Dignifies
The individual disabled
And then its darkness
Is a mature,
Accomplished beauty

The finest beauty,
Issuing a fragrance
That isn't earthly perfume.

I fully contend
With these wonderful things
Emerging
From the state of disability.

How so?
The field scarred
By ploughing
Gives rise
To the best nourishment;

The reed
Separated
From the reed bed
Gives rise to the flute;

And from the mire
And dirt
Emerges the rose:

Pain then,
Gives rise to beauty:
The greater the pain,
The greater the beauty
Arising from it:

If you're disabled,
Hazard your disability,
By sincerely intending
And attempting
To tolerate it,

And by hazarding
The tempestuous ocean,
You will truly emerge
With pearls
From the depths:

Great valuables
Matured by patience,
Which arouses courage,
And a world of kind words,
Each of which is a pearl itself,
And an immense universe
Of kind thoughts,
The roots of a heavenly
Flower bed.

Your life now becomes
The best art,
The finest symphony,
And now something Divine
Is turning the wheels
Of your existence.

The Divine
Enters your life
After you are decisive –
When you take the decision
To be tolerant
And patient
With your disability:

The state of disability
Is ultimately
A Divine state:
The finest human significance
In personality
And beauty.

A LIFE-CHANGING HALF-HOUR

Early this morning,
And way into the day,
I was permeated and suffused
Once again,
By the profound mystery

After decades of daily dissolution,
Perpetually at the interface of difficulty,
How was I to once again,
Once again,
Emerge from the trough?

It seemed, once again,
Insurmountable.

It feels like a complete inhabitation
At a scaffolds edge:

I have to emerge with hope
And optimism,
And I am at my wits end.

It is a predictably tempestuous sea
I am being buffeted in,
And foundering
Is a real possibility.

And I wish to disappear,
Fall asleep,
And in oblivion,
Disappear.
I desperately desire cessation.

But,
Where there is niceness
In an individual,
There are his or her soft-hearted needs
I try to be as nice as I can,
And fully heed
The niceness of others.

At the very least,
A nice personality
Disposes one
To witness hope
And optimism:

As a lucky stroke would have it,
In the throes of woe,
I met a very nice person
In the café late this afternoon

She was of simple personality,
Kind,
And soft-hearted,
And with needs

Most of all,
She feared broken hearts –
Hearts broken by witnessing
And realizing
A failed outcome to the experience
Of difficulties and suffering.

She desired above all,
To witness people
Practicing hope
And optimism
In their trials,
That she may herself be driven to
Practice her heart's desire –
Yet more, yet more affection
And kindness.

Out of her simplicity –
Her sophisticated simplicity,
Out of her niceness,
She moved me,

And I became hopeful,
And was conferred
Something bigger than myself
To live for.
I saw beyond myself
And transcended
My suffering instantly.

And instantly too,
Experiencing her vision,
I myself harboured hope
And optimism,
And affection,
One I fully knew,
After talking to her
And experiencing her beauty,
That I could confer
Upon other people fallen short.

I met this beautiful young woman
Briefly, for about half and hour –
A life changing
Half-an-hour.

She with her great heart,
Brought me from the real,
Yet in the light of expectations,
Unreal world of sorrow,
To inhabit,
Be suffused
And permeated
With the unreal,
Yet very real
World of hope
And optimism.

And now, there are two of us
The number doubled
In our meeting
Of people wanting to express
Affection
Yet more affection –
Myself, and her!

PANACEA

For a long time
Decades even
I neither saw,
Nor witnessed
A way through:

Psychologically,
Physically,
Emotionally,
In feelings,
Intellectually,
And spiritually
I was beleaguered:

My relationships,
Both near and far,
Had foundered;
My scope
Had vanished;
My abilities
Couldn't be purposeful
I strongly knew
That I couldn't apply them
Imminently;
I couldn't work;
And I couldn't educate myself:

Every door
Had shut to me:
But one day,
I discovered clarity
In vision
And witnessing –
By discovering Beauty,
Which is Love.

For, this beautiful world
Has every sign
That it was created with Love.

I had a new beginning
With Beauty
And Love;

And I witnessed
And visualized things
Through Love:
By Love,
And for Love,
And began to think,

Speak
And act
By heart
And mind
With Love:
Empowered with Love
Opened up vistas
In every sphere
Concerning me:
Real living
Was inviting me again,
And I began to live,
And not merely exist.

As I became more knowledgeable
In Love,
I discovered personality,
Character,
And personal attributes,
Mine,
That fully aided and abetted
Living in Love:
Qualities such as patience.

And patiently waiting
More resolution
Inwardly
And outwardly,
My commitment to patience
Resulted in my recovery

From the blights of illness
And disability:

I can now work;
And I can educate myself;
My ability
Can be put to work beneficially
And I possess peace of mind:

Love:
Love, pure and simple,
Is the panacea
For all ills
And ailments,
No matter how prodigious
Or deeply set:

It is Truth that heals;
And that Truth
Can only be Beauty:

The greatest Truth,
And the greatest Beauty,
Is Love!

KINDNESS AND THE TROUBLED

The recipient of kindness
Is empowered with,
And fully deemed
Significant and meaningful -
To have this tremendous significance
And meaning -
To deserve a word
Or act of kindness,
They are worthy of that worthy
Of little children
And animals;

This, the brightest humanly possible speech
And actions
Are reserved for the recipient,
And their experience
Is beautiful,
As deep as is imaginable.

And beauty heals,
Like nothing else.

So, if a person is in difficulty
Or trouble,
The best injection of a remedy
Is to infuse well-being

With the beauty of kindness.

Kindness is the finest beauty
And the kind person
The most beautiful individual.

Both recipient
And benefactor
Of kindness
Are emboldened
And beautified.

The first role of education
Is to empower.
Kindness,
The faculty of kindness,
Shows the most educated individual -
Therefore,
Kindness ought to empower.

And indeed it empowers
The kind person,
And the beneficiary
Of his or her kindness.

The kind person
Brings tidings
From a great realm –
If to call it
A 'heavenly' realm
Is too much
For the secular minded.

The kind person's tongue,
Their hands
Overflow with brightness
From that hallowed realm
From where kindness has its source –
It is the brightest illumination
Humanly possible.
Its comforting words
Are pearls articulated,
Gems brought to bear,
And in their kind actions,
The kind person
Is mantle bearer
Of the deepest universe –
That of little children
And animals.

The kind person
Is a wine-bringer
Plying invaluable liquor,
That brings a cooling brew
For the spiritual edification
Of his or her beneficiary.
The kind person hence
Is in close touch
With the greatest things of the spirit,
And is eminently spiritual.

Their kindness introduces,
Or can re-introduce
The recipient into the world,
Which in turn means
An introduction to the immense world
Of goodness,
Kindness
And love.
Only the most educated can do this.
A kind person has faith
And has the nature of a poet:
The finest understanding.

It is not by outward show,
Or by certificate
That we can truly deem
Someone educated –
It is by their propensity
For kindness.

Nothing that can issue
From a human being
Surpasses kindness.
Therefore,
Being all this,
The kind person
Who is troubled
Possesses every self-conferred
Solace and comfort
He or she needs.

Because of their kindness,
If their desire
Is to pull through,
Their desire
Will receive its satisfaction,
Eminently so.

DRIVING AWAY TURMOIL

Who, outrun by pain
Does to Love turn
Does the finest conduct
Humanly possible discern;

The individual who
Drives away turmoil
With Love and goodness
Possesses the best foil;

The one troubled resorting
To goodness and Love
Has a heart opulent:
With more than enough;

The one by pain fragmented
Is yet more than whole
If he or she practices
Their kindness in heart and soul;

The world belongs to them,
Their exclusive property,
If in tribulation and hurt
They bring Love's prosperity;

The one with no bitterness
Despite a lifetime's adversity
To the humane shows
Utmost, greatest fidelity;

Bitterness never to hurt
By word, thought or deed
Is to reach heaven right now:
To be of little children's creed;

The one hurting and paining
Who does Love multiply
By saying a kind word does
Heaven with energy supply;

I see right before me, truly,
A person in grief and sorrow:
The most beautiful state
From which heaven does borrow;

The one who of a kind word
Is the sincere sayer
Has truly, effectively
Answered God's own prayer;

For blessed him or her
There is no adequate praise
They real ineloquence to beautiful
Eloquence do raise;

In his or her great beauty
I truly witness and see
Someone heaven bound,
And thus, to everything, free!

ADVICE

Lost, and absolutely adrift
On the pathway of life,
Because, steeped in
Convulsive turmoil
Amidst the depth of utter darkness,
You are asked
To possess vision –
To visualize with clarity
A great heart,
A realized, developed mind,
And a terrific vocation –
All whilst utterly disabled
In mind and body.

Your ability to calculate
Has evaporated
And you're asked
To multiply your abilities
And faculties
Embedded as they are in enforced indolence
And intractable retirement.

You feel, incomplete to begin with,
And so, how does one fashion
The clear vision necessary,
And materialize it?

The initial foundation for action
Is patience;
The second is to understand
That your station
Is one of great opportunity;
The third is to acknowledge
That though your inward is dark,
It is entirely beautiful
Because of your good intentions.

The point thus,
Is to illuminate this innate beauty.

Good intentions,
Followed through by good action,
Win you the friendship
Of the world;
For goodness
Is the path of Truth,
And the Truth is welcome to all.

Then, you realize
That in your poverty,
You are rich -
You have wealth within yourself -
Great opulence!

And one of the capstones of this state
Is never giving expression to misgivings -
Forgiveness
And tolerance is uppermost.

And the patience is ongoing -
Which is courage.

You've awoken your heart
And magnified it -
Made it greater!

Without at this stage
Even fully embarking
On the path to recovery
Of your abilities
And faculties,
You are at a tremendous interface -
And this is joy for you.

And you magnify
In greatness now.

Even without the presence of recovery,
Possessed of this self-beautification,
You're a great human being!

THIS MORNING………

This morning,
I was unwell:
I was rendered 'unconscious',
Though nominally awake,
By my condition.

I couldn't fully attend
To your courtesy
And consideration.

As I arrived at consciousness,
I realized well
That you've not judged me,
And understood.

Understanding the unbalanced
Is a poet's gift,
And not judging
Is the sage's gift.

You filled my emptiness
With your thoughtfulness.

It is experiences like these,
That I,
A disabled
And troubled man
Sincerely regard
As peak moments.
I truly wish
That the whole world
Could witness
This very beautiful moment.

However,
The angels look on,
Wondrous!

THE GARDEN.

Deep down, I suppose
I must have had a thirst,
For I was quenched, completely,
To the slake
By pain,
Hurt and sorrow;

Unceasing tears
Streamed from my eyes,
Daily, and for decades;

Yes, I was in a garden,
But there was no sunlight there;
All the fruits it offered,
And in such large measure,
Were copiously bitter
And unwholesome;

How I longed for appetite –
That of my heart,
By avenue of sight –
For blooms which never pale
To be experienced by me.

I had been transformed into ashes.
Nor was there anyone, anyone,
Who even perceived my state,
Let alone understood it –
I was heart burnt withal,
And possessed, fully so,
The sharpest ongoing death.

However, in this state,
One of all-pervasive opacity,
It is easy to witness luminosity
And brilliance.

And I instantly, without the least effort,
Knew completely about light,
I knew, to the slake,
What brilliance really was –
I was eminently qualified
To identify and define it:
It was Love,
Goodness
And kindness.

And I began to revere
Thinking,
Speaking
And acting well.

I revered too,
Those who were well meant,
Who lived virtuously.

Gradually, I began to live
As I embarked on a life of virtue.
And I discovered myself free
Free of fear.
For, those possessed of Truth,
Their fears are diminished.
And since death had already visited me,
I am never to die again.

It isn't trickery, or chance,
That grants freedom,
But cold and deliberate emergence
Into the open,
Boldly facing one's prisons.

I confronted my gaols
By doing my best –
Working hard with the virtues,
Persisting,
Maintaining
At the very least,
A ready smile,
The intention, practiced,
Of offering a handshake.

When I injected Beauty
Into the universe,
I began to grow apart
From my dilemma.
Nothing clears the battlefield
In as exemplary fashion as Beauty.

And the formless within me
Began to take form;
The destitute has a sure dwelling.

I became a bird in soaring flight,
And it is the heart that flies.

And I came to rest
In a garden,
With full blooms exotic,
Never to fade or wither,
And I was to be nourished forever
By Beauty!

Beauty
Is peerless,
Unparalleled,
Substantial
Sustenance!

A POEM FOR YOU MY FRIEND.

My dearest, dearest friend:
you are a kind,
caring,
handsome,
lovely,
and a considerate
and an affectionate person.

Thus, you are constructive
in your attitude,
words,
thoughts
and actions.

Construction is more difficult
than its opposite, being destructive,
and hence you face more difficulties
in being constructive
than in anything not like it.
And you, my friend,
try to build for the better
at all moments –
in all phases and aspects of your life:
privately,
and in your personal life with a partner;
in your work place,

at your leisure
and with everyone else.

This means
that it is with certitude
that you will face difficulties
and problems in your life.
However, with you being committed
to being constructive
with all your heart,
the Unseen forces of the universe
are in accord with you
and fully support you.

Also, consciously and unconsciously
the great in the world are also with you:
the beautiful little children,
the good adults
and the gracious, loving animals.
You are backed up by,
and supported by all this
goodness and beauty,
which is proof of your
own power and strength.

Each and every great force in the universe
loves you,
which makes you strong and powerful.
Contemplate and meditate hard
on your tremendous power and strength -
let it become a true part
of your personality and character -
and then, realizing your power,
you will be ready to act on it.

And you will,
with certainty,
act beautifully in this power -
you will think, speak and act beautifully:
you are committed to goodness after all.

What is your state now then?
What have you become by seeing
through your constructive nature?

You have become a great human being.
And very, very, handsome
and beautiful.

A POEM UPON MEETING A PERSON WHO HAS ENDURED AND DONE THEIR BEST WITH THEIR DISABILITY

The other day,
I met you,
After a decade -

When you witness
The same flower -
The same beautiful flower
After a while,
It has withered a little,
And has, a little, lost its bloom -

You however,
Were fresher,
And more beautiful
Than ever!

TODAY...

Today I met – I truly met
A beautiful person:
She was an ocean of humanity
And beauty:

What rivers of loveliness
Fill her ocean of beautiful personality
And exemplary character?

Care,
Consideration
And concern
Are her vocation –

One moment of her care
Is sufficient to fill the cosmos
With greatness,
And yet, and yet,
Most of her mighty heart
She is still very young –
Has its immense potential
Still to be put to full effect.

How great is her heart then?
She is a nurse.

THE ELECTORATE.

Mining for myself,
I elected myself -
And met others - both electors
And those they elected;

We were all vying for the highest
Seat in the parliament of existence -
Meaning and significance;

Among them
Were those who couldn't elect themselves,
And there were those who couldn't be raised
To the level of electable.
Withdrawn to the margins,
They possessed no manifesto that was
'attractive',
And they were ever-ready to take the oath,
And manage favour -
Yet the race was relinquished from them.

And soon after my own election,
I too became marginalized,
Unelectable,
By myself or the electorate.

And I learnt
That those who are these 'un-electable'
And those who wished to elect them,
But were constrained,
Were the very people of merit
Of significance and meaning
That yes, one ought to mine for oneself,
But not look to the electorate
To ratify significance and meaning
That everyone is elected anyway,
By the great powers of the unseen,
And only oneself can undo oneself of this honour.

Every human being is a mine – of gems,
And it is not another human's say,
Whatever fashion governs them,
To say in order to ratify
What is beautiful,
Great,
Managed in loveliness –
The beautiful,
Great
And lovely
Is self-elected.

YOU: (FOR A CARER)

Your beauty
Is an oil painting

Your goodness
Is the highest creative Art;

Your kindness
Is a genuine child-like trait

And your love
Is Divine.

HAVE FAITH AND PATIENCE!

You are made – recreated – by pain,
Hurt and troubles –

That your life has been sacrificed
To a life-time of difficulties
Can only mean the re-fashioning
And re-making of you –

For you consciously or unconsciously
Placed your neck there where the sword was.
This is courageous – in the extreme
To the point of the finest greatness
And the unseen Universe
can only react affirmatively
And with reward in mind.

You, hence, are close to every Beauty
In that Universe,
Every Majesty
And Greatness.

You have been re-created and re-fashioned
In the mould of utter significance
and meaning.
You will feel your luck gone astray
For the pain and hurt are terrific

But you have received majesty and meaning
The up-lifting and grandeur of you has been realized,
To a degree that cannot be excelled -
You have been beautified beyond measure,
And been bestowed a critical importance
That cannot be bettered

All this lies in the unseen Universe
Which creates and re-creates like
a work of Art
Is fashioned and created
And since the finest Artist
The unseen Universe is re-creating you,
You have become the finest work of Art.

Great works of Art
And the unseen Universe's Art
Is the greatest
Are endless, and bottomless in riches
In knowledge,
Meaning
And significance
And you are this work of great Art
After your trials and tribulations -
Your meaning is endless, bottomless.

Now, think and speak and act carefully –
According to your hallowed station and rank
With goodness, kindness and love
And you will yourself
Complete the work of Art you are
Begun by the unseen Universe.

You lose nothing thus,
By misfortune or difficulty,
But gain –
Have faith and patience –
These are keys to your remedy,
Instantly realized in the moment of pain and hurt.

And instantly,
You are managed,
With its ever power
And strength,
By the unseen.

MUHAMMAD ALI, A WISE MAN
(May God rest his soul)

'Champions are not made in the gymnasium; they are made by a dream, a desire, vision they hold deep inside. Then they need the skill and the will, but the will must be greater than the skill.' (Muhammad Ali in his autobiography, Soul of a Butterfly).

When I was disabled,
With a crippling, demoralizing disability,
My reasoning powers
Saw clearly the impasse I'd been brought to;

I suffered, for reason told me the truth –
That I had a grave disability,
Probably – very likely – to be irrevocable,
And so I was crestfallen
Fallen dead before my death
The suffering was acute, unparalleled,
And since I knew I had to use my reasoning powers
For a solution,
And my reasoning told me
That it itself,
And that I myself

That I had possibly irrevocably
broken down,
I was almost hopeless.

Then I read the words of my hero,
Muhammad Ali, the words above,
And I realized that I'd let my reason lead me
And dominate me
And not my willpower

I realized that my will ought to lead,
And dominate my reason.

I had by realizing this,
And practicing it,
Taken the first step
Of the long journey ahead –
To recovery from my serious disability.
And indeed, so it proved:

My willpower
Allowed me to sustain Love
Above everything else in my life –
I allowed Love to pervade and permeate
My every thought, word and action;
And in tandem I could successfully practice
The difficult art and science of patience –

Thus my willpower led
And dominated my reason.

And now, thirty years later,
I celebrate ten years without serious disability,
And the pain and hurt of being gravely disabled.

Muhammad Ali is a wise man.

My people, resort to wisdom
When troubled and consternated,
Make a life's philosophy out of it,
And practice it - if you then sincerely desire an object,
Or objective,
You will arrive at it in due course,
You will realize it.

A POEM FOR A YOUNG LADY IN A WHEELCHAIR

The sun burns,
And the moon is alone,
Alone, lonely, in the darkness.

The stars,
Are necessarily,
Due to their distance,
Mellow and dim;

You suffer,
And being greater
Than the cosmic bodies,
Your suffering is greater:

Hence, your beauty,
Young lady,
Is greater
Than that of the sun,
Moon
And stars!

Today, when I met you,
You proved to me
Your beauty
A deep,
Profound beauty

Unasked,
You, with every goodwill
And good intent,
Smiled at me –

Do you not have an ample heart,
A majestic mind,
And a great soul?

Do you not possess
The deepest beauty,
Achieved
By simply smiling at me?

SPIRITUALITY, ART AND POETRY.

I was shattered – in every sense
I was woe-begotten – in every way
I was crestfallen – in every hue of being
I was pained – in every manner of thinking
I was wasted – in every meaningful meaning
I was grieved – in every aspect of the inward
I was heartsick – in every route I could take
I was dead – in every desire that
could be fulfilled –
I was friendless – in every avenue
where friends resided;

Yes, I was all this, and more, yet more;

And I needed to be just to my soul
I needed justice for my heart and mind.
Professionals who could assist
And did so ably support
Were the 'lowly' workers
Nurses,
And support workers

At their prompting, I looked at my strengths
And I avidly scrutinized my weaknesses,
I looked at both with a balanced stance,
And sought a medium passage out –

I realized that my most equable moments,
When I discovered equanimity
And self-induced consolation
Were when I thought deeply,
In conjunction with my beliefs
Which were meditating and contemplating
Love, goodness and kindness
My spiritual beliefs.

And I thought at my deepest
When I thought about my own poetry,
Or read that of other poets
When my spirituality was circumjacent
To my poetic necessities.

And I set about emphasizing this discovery,
And gradually the two –
My spirituality and poetic natures blended
And overlapped, as never before.

I realized that true Art informs,
Beautifully so,
That beauty is the core
and essence of true Art,
And that poetry, the great Art,
Is essentially and at heart
spiritual and Divine

In its origin and foundation.

And since beauty is truth,
And truth is beauty,
Poetic thinking pertains to the truth.

Poetic thinking is to realize the cognizant
In relation to effective living,
The realizing of succour
And nourishment for the heart,
Mind and soul
Poetical thinking realizes the opportune,
To be the benefactor of the nectar
Of consolation and comfort.

When the sun of my poetry
Rose in my darkness,
It brought then beauty
For so I am pre-disposed
And the imposed austerity of my suffering
Began to leave my being,
Establishing a core and essence
That I tried to shape and create now,
As immovable and unshakeable.

Thinking deeply,
And successfully so

Is an inerasable, indelible experience,
Particularly when strongly enmeshed
With the finest truth
Goodness, kindness and love.

And so I wrote poetry on these themes.
And I was determined to be persistent
In this pursuit

I comforted others, and myself.
I concentrated hard on my vocation and endeavour,
And I utterly erased the frivolous
And superficial from my makeup,
And was left with gravity and meaning.
I have made no other line since.

And though my debility is recurrent,
I subsequently have instituted
the Art of poetry
And spirituality
In the midst, in the throes of sorrow,
Whenever that reared its head.

When beauty or truth
Is present in one's thinking and
contemplation,
Woe-begotten states begin another demise,
And start to perish again,
On the lovely perilous waters
Of Art, poetry and spirituality,
Whose rocks are liberally strewn
On the water of any untoward storm.

THE ESSENCE AND CORE OF HUMAN EXISTENCE AND PURPOSE

When I was forlorn, reduced,
And disabled,
The ladder of life, living and existence
Was harshly pulled away from me –

As I recovered, in my twenties,
I envisioned my possibilities –
The ladder for scaling was re-instituted,
And opportunities beckoned once more,
These were open to me,
At my behest and were at my command –

Then, unfortunately,
The ladder,
Which at this stage I had somehow re-scaled,
Was violently torn from my grasp
And expectant tread.

But despite this,
I did not choose the errant method or way –

I chose the path of truth,
Which is the path of beauty,
And expressed my deepest essence,
Goodness, kindness and love.

And I have kept to these virtuous practices,
Though greatly disabled –
In range of personality,
And intellect –
Consequently my social skills suffered –

Though I believed in God,
I never fasted, prayed, or went on pilgrimage.

But I think,
Successive living
In good character
Is a lifetime's
Prayer, fasting and pilgrimage –
The whole lot rolled into one.

It is to reach
The essence and core
Of human existence
And human purpose,
The forever, perpetually
Spiritually clement weather:
It is to reach
The unsurpassable.

THE GREAT WOMAN AND MOTHER...

There is great extent
In the power of your beauty

There is great weight,
And gravity
In the wonderful nature
Of your beauty

There is a driven impetus
In the dynamism
Of your active,
Beneficent beauty

There is a great treasure
In the jewel-like character
Of each wondrous aspect
Of your beauty

There is profound and prodigious depth
In the beautiful personality
That shapes
Your momentous beauty

There is ample consideration,
For all,
And everything

In the amazing vision
That ramifies
Through your loving beauty
There is incredible freshness

The lush copious foliage
In the great makeup
You portray as primal in you
As a spring
For the depressed
In your beauty

There is a care,
Cause for concern,
For suffering,
Which is beautified
By the beautiful kindness
Of your beauty

There is a great example
In your incredible selflessness
That accompanies
Your transaction
Of your thoughts and actions
Your beauty

There is a great sacrifice
And the greatest saintliness
In your maturity as a child,
And your regress
To another mature
Child-like state as an adult –

You are made by Beauty
To be beautiful
Forever,
Mother Mary,
Mother Marium.

There is fashioned concrete hope
And majestic achievement
For people in adversity
In your love, goodness and kindness,
A beauty you take,
Always,
To another height of beauty.

COMPLETION.

In the end, the heart:

I have now only my heart to offer –

My heart has softened
As my agony has increased,
As I haven't been able to engage my mind,
And am without volition and impetus.

I have been utterly robbed
Of all ability to act as I would intend.
And yet, I remember love,
And feel it,
And in this remembrance lies
All I have now.

I look upon the disabled,
The agonized
With genuine, sincere empathy
And offer a smile –
I offer a loving heart –
Else, I possess no power.

And yet, my state
Is the state of power,
For it is my sole intention

To be good and kind.

And my inability
To act out,
And word
Goodness and kindness –
Does not leave me bereft –

The completion I have
Lies in my good and kind intentions –

I have no power
Of personality
And character
In the palpable, visible world,
But in my yet immense inner world
At least,
I am complete,
Because of the love I intend
So genuinely
And with sincerity.

PATIENCE…………..

The bud –
Of love,
Of desires fulfilled,
Potential,
Burgeoning ability,
Advanced thought,
Mature learning,
Of creativity,
Of new friendships,
A new social resolve,
Family affairs made original
For, indeed, the first time –
Of consoling,
Of comforting
Of resolution
Of hope bestowing
Of achievement,
Of leadership,
Of true athleticism,
Of completion of mind,
Body,
And the beginning of magnification
Of the heart –
The nourishment of the soul,
Of the making of my particular destiny,
This flowering bud

Began regressing,
And then confined itself,
Bud-like:
What could I do?
The sepals were iron curtains,
And I was veiled
Behind an impregnable prison –

But winter,
Cold arid winter,
Is also an iron-age,
Seemingly all-powerful,
Indelible,
Consolidated,
And confirmed –

But spring – spring
Lies patient,
Waiting with infinite patience,
And is eventually victorious –

The iron bars of the prison
Are rent asunder,
And beauty – yes beauty
Emerges,
And the world is bedecked in hope
Once again –

So too with me -
With infinite,
Bitter patience,
I awaited my spring,
When my bud would burst

My patience,
Nourished
In responsibility
And tact,
And the intelligence
Of the wisdom of patience,
Duly won the day,
And I emerged,
But nascent,
Beginning the climb
To meaning
And significance

But at least
I was flowering,
Blossoming,
Beginning to bloom

I had been offered another,
Improbable chance
In the corrugated patterns of life -
An opportunity,

Once again,
To realize my every facet.

This is a true story.

Patience
Can unlock the impregnable,
Open the tightly closed vault -
From where,
Once dead,
Your remains are resurrected

Patience then,
Is a miracle
Enacted by a fortunate individual,
With fortunate opportunities.

A POEM FOR YOU, AN HONOURABLE BEING.

'A revelation from the Lord of Mercy… …giving good news….'
(The Quran, chapter 41, verses 2 and 4).

The most honourable among mankind,
The wisest men and women,
The greatest individuals
And all the Holy Books
Have recommended
Perseverance,
Persistence,
Willpower
And patience
In order to approximate to,
And come close to the things
We deem most desirable.

Since these qualities are greatly
recommended –
By the greatest people,
And the Holy Books,
They in themselves are great

One of the basis of human greatness
Then is to persist,
Implement one's willpower,
And to persevere
And to be patient.

The person who resolves thus
Has begun their journey into achieving greatness.

Embarking then,
With sincerity,
Accrues every rank,
Every stature
You can be meant to attain –
And yet more.

Therefore, difficulty, trials,
Tribulations and problems
Are not an effacing of your stature,
But a means to enhance it
To its finest height.

Even if you fail to reach the terminus,
Your mere intention,
And the sincere journeying
Will transform you
Into a great individual.

RESPONSIBILITY.

To always be dignified is vital,
The final circumstance achieved.
When it's suffering you face,
Dignity is that you're reprieved.

My great woe, sorrow,
Imposed responsibility -
To myself for others -
The weight of liberty:

But this request,
Was tacit, unspoken,
Almost unacknowledged -
In my battle, it was token;

For I was utterly concerned
With the day to day.
My suffering, my disabilities
Said almost every say -

Leaving little occasion
For momentous vision;
Which I would only realize
When lighted the dark prison

This welcome illumination
Unfolded, and then darkness.
As darkness fell away
To my Art I became witness

For everyone is an artist,
I the poet, aware in thought,
To myself and others
From sorrow's depth brought -

Contemplating deeply,
Upon suffering every day,
I brought perspective,
And thus hope into sway

Contemplation led me
To the deep - to the virtues,
Light in darkness
No one can ever refuse;

And this hope is the vision
Realized. It is the favour
Woe and sorrow conferred
For me and others, to hope savour

All this, all this was gradual,
You have to be prepared to fight,
With love and patience, for decades,
For light will pierce an armoured blight

Consciously, I fought for myself;
Unconsciously, I fought for all
But it was bearing dignity
That allowed spring to grow tall

Whatever you are, or have become,
Remember your dignity
With that majesty in tow,
And patience, you stand for liberty:

When a stand for liberty is taken,
Honestly, and sincerely,
Whether successful or not,
You've stood magnificently

I intended well, I meant well
That is the be all, the end all
The powers-that be then allowed
A shower of significance to fall

I at last realized I'd had vision
In all this miasma and strife,
And by continual battle,
Had given meaning to sorrow, to life!

LOVE…

'That Spring, that of wine hasn't a trace, isn't worthwhile.' **(Hafiz).**

After any difficulty,
Any train of the problematic,
We can expect resolution
We can expect the Spring:

However, if that long-desired Spring
Does not in its wake arouse our love,
Love for ourselves,
And love for the creatures and man,
Then it is a half-measure.

It is essential that we imbibe
that wholesome,
However great our indulging
A great appetite for the wine of love
Will not damage, but exalt
The Spring that does not bring wine
The wine of Love
Isn't worthwhile:

Thus, whatever assistance you receive
For your difficulties and problems,

If its Spring does not lead you
To love yourself and others,
It is but an avoiding short-cut;

For to be without love,
Especially when one has overcome
All manner of issues and trials
Is to waylay one's trajectory in life
It is to avoid that great in yourself
The greatest in yourself

In the relief
Of being relieved of tribulation,
Avail of the tremendous opportunity
before you
To love nature and man,
And if you like, God,
And assume your birth-right:
To behave greatly,
Like a little child.

The state of a little child is the greatest,
Without a shred of doubt;
You become child-like
When you drink the wine of love
When your Spring arrives:
It is due Justice to yourself;

However, how great are you,
If you drink the wine
Whilst in the midst, the throes
Of pain, hurt and sorrow?
Then your worth is incalculable!

Love is the ultimate sanction
And it is self-sanction,
For the appetite for strong drink
Can only come from yourself!

Drink to the slake then,
Wherever you are in life,
For this existence proffers
Nothing greater than drinking wine.

THE EXPERIENCE OF MENTAL ILLNESS

There is the sense,
And the feeling,
Of tremendous difficulty
In mental illness -
Its development and creation
Is difficult to withstand itself -

And real treasure
Is hard to come by,
And, it is still harder
To develop and create.

Hence the location of mental illness
In the human condition
And situation,
Is a critical position
Deserving
The utmost respect and honour.

By ill health,
The client has transcended,
From a nominal
To a great state,
From a person in good health
To a person unwell,
And therefore has a new world to explore,

The world
Of extended,
More valuable patience,
Love,
Goodness,
And kindness.

The client is extended,
Much more,
Much, much more so than ordinarily –

Hence, the mentally ill person
Has within him or her
A tremendous heart,
And their every word,
Thought
And action
Can be vital and crucial,
If they recognize
That they possess a deep heart.

They are no longer
An ordinary member of society,
But someone deeper,
Larger in orbit,
And greater.

Necessarily fashioned
With such burdens and difficulty,
The mentally ill
Are themselves
The treasure of the world.

FOR A WOMAN OF GOOD CHARACTER, WHO IS RESIGNED TO HER DISABILITY AND ENDURES IT TO THE BEST OF HER ABILITY

As I see you,
With your lovely face,
And majestic eyes,
My heart and soul
Are involuntarily drawn
To the deep flow of beauty,
From deep inside you –

So, I begin to witness clearly
Your great heart,
Filled with love,
Goodness
And kindness,
A heart
Once avidly,
And right now,
Reduced
By pain and hurt,
That arose out of debris,
And re-created itself,
By retaining its beauty.

And this is real beauty -
To lose
What one considers valuable,
Indispensable,
And yet remain alive
To good character.
This thus, is the great heart,
And greatness is beauty,
A beauty
To be recognized
And felt by our hearts
And souls.

Your love,
Goodness
And kindness
Are now precious,
And you are more valuable
Than all the gold and diamonds
In the world.

To be so valuable,
Is that not to be great -
And beautiful?

FOR A CONSCIENTIOUS YOUNG PERSON FACING DISABILITY.

The waves
Of the Great Ocean
Have reached their shore –
They have alighted upon you,
In your youth.

The Great Ocean
Is the world of Beauty
And Handsomeness,
Of tremendous opportunity,
And wonderful aspiration:

The world is your oyster,
For you to shape
To your wont
And desire.

Your kindness
Is the instant flowering
Of a seed of your heart
Instant flowering,
Which is a miracle;

Your mind is magnificent
Its intentions,
And your heart
Made brilliant
By your mind's reflections.

Thus, your heart,
Enhanced
And driven
By a majestic mind,
Leads you with its courage
Into realms of greatness.

You possess optimism
And true faith,
For you believe in kindness.

The elixir,
The summit
Of your existence
As a young person
Is when you practice kindness
By thought,
Word
And deed.

There is no finer example
You can set,
Nothing better to institute
Towards young
Or old.

If this is the ploughing
Of your youth,
Your condition
As a young person,
I wonder
At the wondrous:
How marvellous
Will the harvesting be?

ON FACING DIFFICULTY...

'He (or she) who knocks persistently ends by entering.' (Imam Ali ibn Abu Talib).

All things come to those who wait.

Balance
Sometimes even nominal
In difficulty
Is a precarious venture

To be bereft
Of replies, even repartee,
For the situation
Is so demanding
That it is impossible to countervail,
And many a time,
To be bankrupt
In ability
And acumen –
Now effaced,
Or masked in your being,
And then to effectively plan
Balance,
Is most onerous.

Sometimes,
You're asked for courage –
When courage
And the means to evoke it
And practice it have been masked –
It is an excruciatingly arduous task
Achieving balance.

But the sincere intention to achieve balance,
And a positive practical movement
Towards realizing it
Are the thin end of the wedge
Into its ultimate realization.

When a person is adamant in demand –
Particularly with that noble,
And wholesome,
Such as a desire
To emerge from the darkness
Of the implication of disability,
Or illness and its residues
Is a particularly complete
And great desire,
And shows patient resolve
In persisting,
He or she stands to succeed
In their honourable quest.

Patience,
And persistence
In maintaining
The state of engagement
Are the keys
To opening the door
To the garden of balance.

This achievement effaces
All gone before,
By way of disability,
And its ramifications
For the individual
As an individual,
And as a member of society,
As well as the meaning
Of serious illness,
And is a renewing of that personality.

However,
The renewal of the personality
Does not wait till the end
Of one's period of patient resistance
It gradually seeps into character
And personality
During the journey

This makes for a formidable individual,
And thus your strength of character
Is tremendously enhanced:

Be patient,
And persistent
In pursuing you goal.
All things come to those who wait.
The fruits of patience are sweet indeed!

I TELL OF A STORY...

I tell of a full and completed story
Of hurt,
Pain
And sorrow –

I was the moth,
At whose feet the world lay,
That was immolated:
It was written as inevitable
In my fate –
On the candle of grief:

And it seemed, to all scrutiny
To be continuous,
Permanent –
A sleep
Never to be woken from,
An ambitious state of slumber.

Yet each pain, in my experience
Has hidden within it
A deep, blessed secret –
A valuable secret
I partake of, unconsciously,
A mystery rich,
Within my being

From the onset of my difficulties.

My heart, in its demise,
Has dwelled in regions remote:
Remote from myself –

My soul felt the pain,
Indeed that acute, dire pain
Was its only nourishment;

There was a raging fire in my breast;
And all the while,
The beautiful secret within me
Was alive, living, thriving!

I instinctively, truthfully,
Knew my duty –
This was an inerasable fact
Of my heart and mind and soul.

My duty was to be responsible
In word,
Deed
And thought.

Unconsciously
I was eliciting a serious opposition
To my grave issues:
And I continued imparting my duty
For decades.

Then suddenly, unannounced,
One day, the cloud lifted.
I discovered
I could think,
I could imagine vividly:
I could write!
I could allow my imagination
A fruitful carte blanche
And I could decree the fruits
Of my contemplation
And meditation
To others facing problems
And lead them out of their problems.

What could be greater?
What could be greater outcome
Of decades of dissolution
Than to be in a position
To help and assist your fellows
To overcome their issues

So definitely and ably so
The finest honour
Anyone is capable of receiving
And I'd been honoured thus.

This was the wonderful secret lodged
And sequestered deep in my breast,
That was born in me,
And brought to immediate effect
The very moment
I was initiated and introduced to difficulty
And trauma.

This is a worthwhile journey,
A worthwhile story
I have told here.

Mine's is a beautiful tale.
A story has a beginning,
A beautiful narrative,
A beautiful ending
And a magnificent sequel.

All these are achieved,
In one fell swoop,
Right at the story's beginning,

At the onset,
When you decree,
Amidst particular difficulty,
To practice being responsible,
For the rose blossomed,
Is beautiful,
But its beauty
Is innate, is fully contained
In its seed.

Wonders,
Beautiful wonders
Are in their initial instigation,
At the starting block,
For that first stage
Is a wonder in itself.

GOODWILL.

I am silenced,
By my predicament,
But I rise up, in heart still;

I am very hurt
By my dilemmas,
But I try to ascertain a state beyond,
I try to transcend
My sorrow with goodness;

I am set apart,
Irrevocably,
From my fellows,
By unanswered prayers,
But I still implicate the beauty
Of friendship;

I am constantly awash,
Bathed
In being awry,
In mind, heart and soul,
But I am trusting still;

I well know
To the slake
Multitudinous difficulties,

But I still, with pleasure,
Practice every goodness
And am free of envy;
I am eternally cast onto the stage
Of intellectual poverty,
But my wealth is my sincere attempt
At creative thought and contemplation;

I have naught;
I have naught to bestow
That can be acquired mentally,
But I proffer,
With all my heart,
Kindness to all;

I, the strong one,
Who could once
Make a recipient drunk with my love,
Can only offer a sip
Of loving today;
But that loving is yet potent!
That one sip
Has matured,
Like the best wine,
In vats in darkness
And solitude:

And I have no fear of shame,
For despite my levelling
By the wholly problematic
What passed beyond bounds
In difficulty and tribulation
I made temperate with goodwill:
And, practicing that goodwill, brought joy!

BEAUTY AND TRUTH...

To encounter,
And to be embraced
By the intransigent,
The unavailing,
The immoveable fixity -
That keeps one rooted,
Impaled to one locus,
Without issue
And meaning -

And with every inevitable hour,
And arriving day
Moored to ungenerosity
And moreover, regress:
What is the essential nature
Of this impasse?

This is the dwelling
Of heart
And mind
Of those hidden from view
And it was necessary,
And imperative
That they be observed
Viewed
To be open to appreciation:

This is those released,
Given absolute liberty
In order to be incarcerated,
Those taken by the hand
To their grave,
A deep burial,
In which their awareness is intact
And acute:

This, then, becomes
The state of lifelessness.

And still, and yet,
Much now
Is exposed to their vision
And view,
And hand –
Learning,
Significant attainment
By intellectual endeavour –

A whole sea is available to them,
In one mere cup
Of the moment
Of self-appreciation,
But cannot remotely, remotely,
Quench their thirst:

Their woe knows no end,
And their tears are unceasing.

Yet, and yet,
There is Beauty –
The Truth that is:
'Beauty is Truth,
'And Truth is Beauty.'

Beauty is a garden,
At the very least.

A shady garden,
And its leafy splendour
Belongs to you.
And you can drink the wine
Of real life
Into yourself,
To revive yourself.

You, once turned to ashes,
An occasion that produced the much desired
Addition to the garden's soil,
To its potential,
Yielding to an ever-fresh freedom:
Your whole life now
A field of blooms exotic.

Enter this garden,
Till and plough its soil
The toil and hard work
Is worth the trouble.
The blossoms
Cannot pale.

You have forged Love
With all this,
And now your soul
Won't taste death.

'Beauty is Truth and
'Truth is Beauty.'

When you face hardship,
The sweetest cordial
You can drink is the Truth:
The great Truth of Love.

This Love implies friendship,
Empathy,
The tremendous ability to offer
Solace and comfort,
The Truth of the ability to take thought,
And imagine:
To be creative;

The Truth of the great gift of charity
If any of these Truths
Are present in your life,
You are yet blessed
With good fortune.

To feel Love,
And still more,
To give it,
Alone are great blessings.

Hardship empties you
That you may be filled with Love
And these great Truths.

Your thinking,
Contemplation
And meditation
Are now creative –
Ultimately creative,
For they in turn
Foster Truth
In your social environment;

And by successive degrees,
Your ability to portray the Truth
Will increase in intensity:

Perhaps your agony
Had been created
For this eventuality –
That you most meaningfully,
And with the finest significance
Avail of this Beauty –
The Truth –
Of Love
And very other Truth:
And every other Beauty!

FEAR AND JOY: I DO NOT FEAR!

I fear the inevitable onset
Of difficulty
For it could become a labyrinth
With no exit;

I fear
The pain of difficulty
For it could become the inevitable
The hurting
That knows no avenue
Into peace of mind;

I fear dwelling
In the world –
For it may inevitably be
That the world's pain
Will penetrate
And permeate
My defences
And lodge
Permanently
In my heart.

I fear
Being bereft of knowledge
For it is only a learned mind

And heart
That can safely navigate
The rock-strewn waters
Of difficulty.

But, I do not fear!

For I know,
Every difficulty,
In the manifold variety
In which it may manifest
Is fully encompassed
And surpassed
By goodness,
Kindness
And love.

And whilst difficulty
May be of a long duration,
It is yet a temporary phenomenon:

I know with certitude
That goodness, kindness and love
Are immortal
And outlive
Every undesired
Aspect of the world
Brought to bear

By anyone
Or anything.

Goodness, kindness and love
Will win, thoroughly,
Completely,
Against the pain-filled
Game of the universe
In the end:

What fear then I?

The great expectations
I have of goodness,
Kindness
And love
Are so keen-edged
And sharp,
They cleave my difficulty,
Its hurt and pain:

Virtue thus proves itself
The most strong,
Robust
And durable
Of all things in the universe:

There is therefore,
Nothing stronger
Than the good, kind and loving:

This fact confers the hope I need,
To transcend the pain,
Hurt, bewilderment and trap
Of adversity.
Love, goodness and kindness
Are lights that outshine
Any possible darkness.

LOVE...

I saw difficulty and trial
As the ultimate bier
That took me to Love –
To Truth's majesty, and tier:

For Love truly heals
Every, every ailment,
And is the sure answer
To every predicament:

Love is dashing answer
To each and every sorrow:
Love's wealth is truly yours
Riches you needn't borrow:

And Love is everywhere –
It is truly, everywhere –
In infinite copious amounts,
Working with every flair:

Love is the beautiful flower
Of sorrow's great seed
That satisfies all, always,
Satisfying every creed:

Love is *the* religion, *the*
One of the thoughtful
And it is so majestic,
Taken up, you're successful:

So Love can resolutely
And really heal your hurt,
Love's the wear – inner and
Outer – the best worn shirt:

When Love comes to you,
You are inhabiting spring –
For it bedecks hearts with joy
And transforms suffering:

Love is the best answer
To trial by tragedy
Its transformation is that
Again, for life you're ready:

The library of the thinker
Has Love's great Book,
And you needn't read it all –
One glance suffices, one look:

If a limited word - Love -
Within it is everything great
You can do anything -
Give yourself scope and spate:

My fellow adults and children,
Only Love is to be followed,
Everything by it to be designed,
Fashioned, coloured and contoured:

Love is more than symbol -
It is greatness and in action,
Great is its healing power -
You need of it but a fraction:

A drop of Love is the Ocean
Of Love: no matter how small,
It is everything to everything -
To all on earth and heaven it is all:

The most beautiful Love
Is found in its every form,
Every variety of Beauty
Love can never be uniform:

Love yourselves, and you will
Draw Love from the Unseen,
The deepest source of Beauty,
Most effective and most keen:

Love is panacea,
Love is remedy,
That stands always,
Awaiting, ever-ready:

I embraced Love
When in difficulty,
And I discovered Love –
Made to cure humanity:

I saw difficulty and trial
As the ultimate bier –
That took me to Love – to
Truth's majesty, without fear!

JOURNEY IN SINCERITY

The key, the route,
To everything worthwhile
Is sincerity;

How does an afflicted person,
Facing trial,
Gravitate
To a steady posture,
A firm stance,
In which he or she is ready
To act positively?

Acting positively
Is steadiness,
And firmness.

The first stage
Is to arrive at the driving seat,
In order to confront –
Come face-to-face
With your adversity:

The key, the pathway,
Is to be sincere,
Sincere, always.

With meaning,
every steady posture,
every firm stance
Must visualize Love –
This is the vision true,
And so, your thoughts,
Words and actions
Have to be in accord
With this desire.

One has to think well,
Speak well
And act well.

Thereby,
Harmony
Can be best established
With one's dimensions –
One's inner and outer
Nature,
And with people and things.

Forgiveness
Has to be in place;
And forgiving oneself
And the asking of forgiveness.

Clean the slate.
This is the first stage of Love.
Forgiving
Is one of the finest acts of Love.

The state one creates
Is the one
That needs never to negate
Anything good done for us,
How-so-ever small:
To regard as tremendous
Every niceness,
Anything worthy
That has happened to you,
No matter how 'slight'.

Do your best to do this.
Expend effort for gratitude.

Moreover,
Remember you're worthy
Of the Love
Of animals,
Children,
Good adults.

Love is so estimable,
It is the greatest prize:
And you are worthy of it.

Now, you are in the driving seat.
Love is yours,
So you lack nothing,
By way of worthiness
And self-esteem –
And now you're eminently estimable,
And re-conferred the stature
To confront
Your tribulation.

You have now, also, the capacity
After the foregoing training,
Kindness to yourself –
To be courageous,
And hence to be patient.

Be patient,
It is true brilliance
Truly enacted.

Seek out help.
Keep the good.
Leave out the bad.
And since you've been sincere

In all these endeavours,
You have reached the state of Truth,
Which is Beauty,
And which is Love.

Whilst you may not have overcome
Your problems
And difficulties,
Because the state of Truth,
Which you now hold,
Is Beauty,
Or Love,
It is the state of human triumph.
And yet, your troubles
May not have evaporated:
You yet face trial.
It is stark,
And most real.
And you think that this state
Is yet and still dark, lowly and bare.

You think that the state of brightness
Is yet and still aloof,
That your world isn't bright
And that you are unjustly denied
Your lamp-like attributes;

However,
You are now level
With the earth,
The originator of the rose,
The creator of nourishment,
The solid foundation
Of beautiful homes,
The immovable surface,
That allowed the tread
Of many a fantastic romance,
The suitable home of animals
A place where dreams come true.

Now, level with this loveliness,
You are level with Beauty,
Which is Truth,
Which is Love.
You are face-to face
With greatness –
And you are as 'lowly' as the earth.
And your state is that of greatness.

You are great now……..
…….within your trial.

**Where there is sincerity,
There is no stage
In trial and tribulation
Beginning,
Middle,
Or end,
That can ever be deemed
Negligible,
A waste,
Meaningless,
Profitless,
And without mature and rich
Significance.**

AS LONG AS YOU LOVE...

Despair,
In the beginning,
Is a vehicle
Embarked upon
That takes your personality
To your desired destination.

But it is up to you,
To make sure the vehicle
Is in good repair,
And well stocked with oil,
And fuel.

The tyres
Will be vulnerable
On the thorn strewn road,
And it is up to you
To have repair kits in reserve.

But even if despair
Is there at the end,
At the terminus
Of your journey,
You've succeeded
In one fell-swoop

By deciding upon Love:

By deciding upon Love
Right at the beginning,
At the point of embarking.

It may be:
Despair at the beginning,
Despair at the end:

It does not matter,
As long as you Love!

For Love is the nectar,
Nay the transformed nectar,
The trophy-condition,
The elixir of triumph
That is beyond, way beyond
All conceivable majesty
And magnificence
The mortal mind can imagine,
A most improbable creation,
Beyond the angelic,
Saintly,
Or Prophetic universe
To conceive of.

It is the most valuable entity
In the universe,
And the greatest.

The state of love,
Achieved, is best;
The state of admixture of love and despair
Is less perfectly situated
In one's being,
But the content of love therein
Constantly strengthens you,
Making the despair a veritable backdrop,
And thus, you at least transcend despair:

Thus love,
That purity and perfection
Is the best quality to harbour
Within one's being:
It means that one cannot be be-spoilt!

TO MY FELLOW AFFLICTED SOULS...

To trading blows
With the tidings and results
Of affliction,
I am a dab-hand;

To attending,
Fully sentient,
My own funeral,
Witnessing myself
Wholly dead
In a daily
And perennial manner
I am habituated;

But, I do all this, with Love.

Love softens
The blows taken;
Love resurrects me;

And so, I stand steadfast,
To, by and in Love:
It brings grandeur
To my dealings.

And so,
I acquire the appropriate state
To harvest
All the fruits of life:
I am invited
To the side of friendship;
I am granted
The faculty of forgiveness,
And my every thought
Is a prayer.

Explanation?

To live by Love
Is to live by Power,
Beauty
And Truth
It is to live truly

This true living
Only transpires
After the momentous
Has been experienced,
And established –

And the momentous

Is to have come face-to-face
With adversity,
To constantly stand
Steadfast to it,
And to tolerate
Your demise
With good character:
Thus you are established
In this world.
Will you not then be granted
The faculty to forgive?
Great capacity for friendship?
And the ability
To take tremendous thought?

And the apex,
The summit
Of tremendous thought
Is when it seems a prayer.

The moral is,
My fellow afflicted souls,
To decide on Love.
To decide on Love
Is to hold it in one's hands,
As yours, so to speak.

**To be able to call
Love one's own,
To use it as one wills,
Precious,
Infinitely precious Love,
Is that not to be empowered?
Is it not a dream world?**

**Love is so great,
Great is the beneficiary of Love
Great is the benefactor of Love.**

THE MEANING OF SUFFERING...

You attained
to the rank
of suffering -
a hallowed station –
for that is the hidden Road
of Prophets,
saints
and mothers,
giving rise
to the greatest Beauty.

Suffering
is the robe of honour,
and wrapped in it,
you are the very insignia,
the very emblem
of greatness,
for then you really live,
and those who really,
truly live
are the great.

The meanings of suffering
are multitudinous,
infinite,
so much is contained
within the state of suffering
that you are the greatest poem
or greatest work of Art.
And those dignified
in their suffering transmit
an already elevated state
to ultimate transcendence –
to the spiritual:
for, to be responsible
in thought,
word
and deed –
in accord with decorum,
is to go beyond the angels,
who do not suffer.

To be of good character
when suffering then,
is the greatest possible attainment –
for that is the distilled essence
of the humane,
the greatness of humanity,
the state of childhood:

For children,
sentient
and intelligent,
centre stage
in our troubled world
are good,
kind
and loving:

Suffering hence,
isn't bitter,
but very great!

And greatness
Is sweetness!

THE LAKE THAT BECOMES THE OCEAN

I had suffering,
Woeful suffering
Inflicted upon me
Early in life –
And its gathering, condensing
Did not abate,
Or take time to catch breath;

My heart
Was in intransigence held,
As world when in grip of winter,
Unshakeably clothed.

Hence I was convinced,
Even then,
That everything is seasonal
And has a season,
No less sorrow and grief.

The dissolution of decades,
Meant that my tears
Had become a lake,
A haven for flora and fauna,
And a source of hope.

I had wept however,

Taking thought,
The one complemented the other
And in significance I rose
And meaning achieved –
A state one discovered
Interesting and useful to others.

And thus I had given rise
To a plethora of thinking –
I generated contemplation,
For the shrubs and waterfowl
That bedecked the lake of my tears
Were my colourful creation,
And having been their source
In being created,
Were stimuli
To the heart and mind.

Time and events are permanent;
The precipitation was a perpetual entity,
But life teemed because of me.

The grindstone of suffering
Produced music
And I gave new garments
For people to wear:

In their winters
I gave vocation –
To the suffering of others –
To rise,
And, embracing Beauty,
Bedeck the world
With their goodness.

The desert
Was made green
And green it remained,
Though winters visited it,
Inevitably so,
Perpetually so.
The winters may seem to dominate,
But this is seeming –
In reality,
A wholesale Spring
Has replaced them.

Winter is the face
The unreal world has to show
To be itself.
The truth,
The reality is,
Spring bedecks everything

Within sight,
Or hidden from view
And those who accept this Spring
Partake of it beautifully.

If a drop of Love,
When it joins the Ocean
Becomes the Ocean,
What does a lake of Love
Become,
When it joins the Ocean?

ALL IS ONE COMPENDIUM

Difficulties
Are one compendium –
One affliction
Of heart
And mind,
Adversity in enabling
Worldly manner,
And creating pain
For loved ones.

But difficulties
Are another *one* compendium –
A great,
Beautiful,
Poetic vista –
A realization
Of a blossomed
Heart
And mind.

And this, being a permanent blossom,
Is a heavenly entity.

How so?

If it is Truth that you revere,

Know that Truth is Beauty.
That affliction,
And its resolutions,
Being compendiums,
Are from one locus,
Respectively.

Thus the Truth is one,
And Beauty a Unity:
Spring is one whole:

And Beauty itself
Can only emerge from Beauty –
The one seed of Beauty
Contains all of flourished Beauty.

Difficulty is beautiful,
Because it is resolved by beauty.
Therefore, the beautiful is difficulty,
Giving rise to the beautiful resolution.

If thus, you witness
Your difficulty as Beauty
And Truth,
You know with certitude
That it is special,
And especially made for you,
For your benefit.

This knowledge
Enables patience
And steadfastness,
It enables tolerance.
It enables good character
In the midst of difficulties.

Patience,
Steadfastness,
Tolerance
And good character
Are the witnessing
Of the one seed of difficulty,
The seed of Beauty.

And this is a wonderful tending
Of the growing blossom,
The best gardening:

Will not the finest,
Most beautiful
Blossoming result?

And, because the seed is Truth,
It gives rise to
The most precious Beauty –
A resurrected,
Immortal wonder!

Wondrous hence,
Are your sincere dealings
With difficulties,
A wonder that tells you
To embrace the moment
Of trial and tribulation
As a precious stepping stone
To beauty,
And greatness.

Trials, tribulations
And difficulties
Are not then obstacles
In your path,
Are rich stepping stones
To every human wonder!

Try to, with sincerity,
To, as much as you can,
Embrace the opportunity
Of difficulties -
And with this embrace
At the outset,
You are poised
For unparalleled success,
Unprecedented achievements!

THANK YOU!

'INVITE THE DIVINE'

POEMS

ASPECTS OF THE HEART
SERIES VOL 24
DIFFICULTY AND THEN, JOY

SHAKIL A I DAWOOD

KINDLE DIRECT PUBLISHING

BOOKS BY SHAKIL A I DAWOOD

THE 500 COMPLETE TWO LINE POEMS

A SPEAR OF GRASS POETRY

IN CONTEMPLATION SELECTED POETRY

GRIEF AND GOD

THE HAIRDRESSERS SALON

A SPIRITUAL ANTIDOTE TO DEPRESSION

KALAM THE PEN

OBSERVATIONS: A LIFE EXPERIENCED

IMMERSIONS POEMS

THE VERSE GARLANDS

GOODNESS KINDNESS AND LOVE

ASPECTS OF THE HEART VOL 1

ASPECTS OF THE HEART VOL 2

'WORDS' ESSAYS ON LIVING WITH SCHIZOPHRENIA

WITNESSING – MESSAGES OF HOPE

THE CAFÉ OF LOVE SELECTED POETRY

BOOKS BY SHAKIL A I DAWOOD

'Immersions, The Poetry of Schizophrenia and Psychosis' Volumes I and 2

'Solace in a Maelstrom, Conversations with God'

'Art Therapy for Schizophrenia, A Novel Approach'

'Observations of the Prophets: Their Characters and Personalities'

'Revolutionary Poems, An Effective Guide to Non-Violent Insurrection'

WITH THANKS TO KINDLE DIRECT PUBLISHING

YH YMm YAMkm

www.ingramcontent.com/pod-product-compliance
Lightning Source LLC
LaVergne TN
LVHW050553160826
845677LV00011B/2294

* 9 7 9 8 4 0 9 5 6 8 4 5 0 *